Girl Fighting Exposed

Dean Henryson, LCSW

ISBN: **1493767496**
ISBN-13: **978-1493767496**
6th edition

DEDICATED

to
Jackie

CONTENTS

ACKNOWLEDGMENTS

My college instructors and teachers
throughout my life.

1 INTRODUCTION

Bear in mind that fighting is animalistic behavior.

Some people may be uncomfortable with such revelations, as humans are often not portrayed in this light. This is especially true in regards to girls.

Although we have attained a more realistic perspective over the last few decades, our culture still has difficulty identifying girls too far outside of loving, innocent, and nurturing people.

But girls are observing and being exposed to more physical violence among females than in previous generations. The phenomenon of girl fights deserves careful attention and understanding.

Let's consider an imaginary example of a girl who we will call Jenna. She has an ex-friend who spreads rumors that she is a slut.

Besides the hurt, what other emotions do you think she might feel?

When any person experiences a hurt or loss, they feel vulnerable and powerless. Anger comes as an attempt to stop the hurtful conditions. It is frequently directed at others, especially if they are perceived as the cause.

Jenna's initial tactics to deal with this hurt may be devious angry actions. These may include socially ostracizing the girl, "accidentally" bumping into her in the hallway, or spreading lies about her.

Jenna may also directly confront her adversary.

Anger exerts strength as an attempt to gain power over the loss. Becoming dominate/powerful is the goal.

The higher the level of anger, the more adrenaline is pumped through the body to increase physical strength. Endorphins are created to reduce physical pain. Blood pressure and blood sugar levels are increased. Heart rate and breathing accelerate. Pupils dilate.

The body is preparing to either fight or run, otherwise known as the fight or flight response.

Blood is actually diverted out of the higher functioning parts of the brain and into the body's muscles. This sugar and oxygen enriched blood gives people more muscular power, but the higher functioning parts of their brains are compromised.

With this decreased intellectual functioning, when words or manipulative tactics do not beget enough power, some girls choose to get physical. This usually involves punching, kicking, and pulling hair.

Controlling your adversary's very body comes into play.

These animalistic responses have been cued up physiologically and become more natural to the girls than before they were angry.

Generally, females have less muscle mass than males, especially in the upper body. So an average girl throws less damaging punches and kicks as opposed to an average guy. This means that incapacitating your enemy with a good pin is more essential in girl fights if you want to inflict a lot of damage.

This was especially important and probably an instinct that evolved during much less civilized times, when a girl had to kill, severely injure, or submit her enemy to survive.

When the two girls fall to the ground, a natural battle for getting on top begins.

Between two inexperienced female fighters— which defines the majority of women—pinning the other on her back by sitting on and straddling her is the most dominate/powerful position. Both fighters strive for a dominate position to minimize their injuries and maximize power over their opponent.

Due to her inexperience, the girl on the bottom is usually unable to dislodge her adversary. She is in a state of vulnerability and loss of movement.

Before this pin occurs, friends in the crowd may even yell, "Jump on top of her," "Get on her," or "Sit on her," intuitively knowing this is a stronger place to be.

If one girl is already pinned, the top girl's friends may yell, "Don't let her up!" or "Keep her down!" displaying their belief of her advantageous position.

Friends of the bottom girl may yell, "Get up!" or they may immediately attempt to help their friend, showing their belief that she is in trouble.

Their belief has truth to it.

Simple with regards to physics, the pin works better in female fights as opposed to male fights.

Because women are generally shorter than men, the top girl will usually have a lower center of mass than the same position taken in a guy fight. This lower center of mass means that she is more stable and balanced on the bottom victim. (Think of how a low sports car is more stable around corners compared to a raised four by four truck.)

In addition, female hips are much larger in proportion to their bodies as opposed to male hips. This means that on average they cover more of the bottom girl's body in comparison to the same position taken in a male fight. So a girl sitting on top has her weight distributed over a greater portion of her opponent's body, and creates a wider base of support for herself. This means greater stability for her and more difficulty for the bottom girl to move out of the pin. (Think of a triangle's stability verses a rectangle's.)

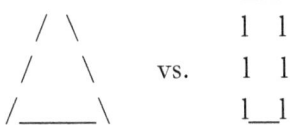

This type of pin is sought naturally, and over time it has been endowed with its own name, *the schoolgirl pin*, in addition to its formal name in martial arts, *the mount position*.

It is one of the most common pins and submission techniques used in an inexperienced girl fight.

Some girls are fearful of it to the point that they avoid fighting another female who may win this favorable position.

The girl on top may do additional acts to force submission. These involve demonstrations of power, inflicting more pain or loss to the pinned girl.

Once in submission, the bottom girl will continue in this state even after the fight. She strives to avoid the powerless situation of being dominated from reoccurring. Though for this to occur, she must have been in true submission, not faked.

This dynamic even occurs with canines. In an effort to establish hierarchy in a pack or correct a pack member, a dominant dog will keep another dog pinned on its back until it becomes submissive.

The struggle between the girls is a primal, animalistic one. As such, it uses animalistic dynamics.

However, because of humans' greater intelligence, these instinctual dynamics for dominance drift into the psychological realm more than in the animal kingdom.

This psychological brew with physical struggle is explored in detail.

Although some of this enlightenment may be new and uncomfortable to readers, censoring is not exercised so as to provide a greater understanding.

2 PHYSICAL ADVANTAGES

The girl on top benefits simply from her position.

Gravity works for her. It constantly holds her opponent down and holds her body on her opponent.

Gravity also accelerates her punches down. In contrast, the pinned girl's punches are weakened by this force pulling them down even before they are thrown.

The girl on the bottom often tries to sit up, but this is easily thwarted by the other girl pushing her back down or moving further up on her. Her failing attempts tire her neck and stomach muscles.

Being on her back, the bottom girl loses the ability to use her arms to push herself off the ground or to use her legs to raise herself onto her knees. She is similar to a turtle on its back. Arms and legs flail about, without much effect.

These physical handicaps play on her mind. Fear,

desperation, and insecurity grow.

She may try to bridge, which involves thrusting her hips up to throw off the top girl. But with inexperienced fighters, this is often aborted after her opponent's body lunges threateningly towards her head.

The top girl is able to protect her body with her hands and arms better than her opponent. Because her knees and thighs are crowding her opponent's arm movement, and because the ground further restricts this arm movement, her opponent cannot protect vulnerable areas as well.

But more than just that, the bottom girl's position acts on the *minds* of both girls (more on this in psychological advantages chapter). The bottom girl feels more vulnerable, and the top girl feels tougher.

The bottom girl may pretend not to care that she's pinned, just to psychologically attempt to eliminate the powerlessness of her position. But this mental defense cannot last.

With little effort, the top girl can immobilize her opponent's arms. She may use her hands to pin them to the ground. Or if she maneuvers her shins over the bottom girl's arms, she incapacitates them.

She is then free to punch or gouge at the eyes of the other. She can even use the ground as her weapon, slamming the other girl's head into it.

One or both of the bottom girl's arms may also be pinned against her own body by her adversary's thighs or buttocks. The top girl also can wedge the bottom girl's arms between her calf and thigh, incapacitating them.

Besides these actions restricting arm movement, blood nourishing the arm muscles can decrease. The arteries can be compressed along the inside of her upper arms.

The bottom girl lacks all of these debilitating options. The top girl may even confidently taunt, "Now what?" "What now?" or "What're you gonna do now? Huh?" to emphasize the bottom girl's latest loss of arm motion.

Some girls never imagined that this level of immobility were possible. They are shocked when pinned in this way. It never occurred to them that this totally submissive position could happen to them, and they give up fighting almost immediately.

This freeze response may be a final attempt to stop the top girl from continuing to fight.

The top girl, like a baseball pitcher, can move her fist back behind her head and throw it at the bottom girl's head with more velocity and force. She can use her body to add force to each punch by raising it up and letting it drop down with the punch to add momentum. She can curl her stomach muscles as the punch travels to further increase its strength.

With every punch the top girl throws into the bottom girl, the ground prevents the bottom girl from moving backward. This makes each impact more destructive. In contrast, the top girl can move back *with* the bottom's girl's punches, decreasing the energy of their impact.

If the bottom girl's arms are not pinned down, both girls have the option to choke each other with their hands. However, the top girl can hold this position better by pinning her adversary's neck against the ground. She can easily break a choke hold on herself by leaning back or rising on her knees just a few inches.

The bottom girl has some leg movement, but often fails to utilize this to any advantage.

Her head movement is blocked from behind and may be further confined if caught between the top girl's thighs. This increases her vulnerability to punches to the face, choking, scratches or pokes to the eyes, and hair pulling. Head movement may also be compromised if the top girl's knees rest on the other girl's hair.

In a play fight, the top girl may use her hands to try to close the bottom girl's nose and mouth to playfully tease her vulnerability. In a serious fight, the top girl may stuff mud into these orifices or hit them with a rock. If a puddle is nearby, she may push the bottom girl's nose underneath it. Or if an object is pushed into the bottom girl's mouth and touches her uvula, she may reflexively vomit and fear drowning or choking in this vomit.

Her clothes may be ripped or pulled, revealing private parts to bystanders and causing humiliation. The bottom girl lacks physical freedom, making it more difficult to prevent this and to reciprocate this on her opponent.

If she wears a skirt, she is already in a revealing position and subject to humiliation and jeers from the crowd. This is another difference between girl versus guy fights. Also, girls have two private areas which can be revealed versus guys' single private area.

The front of a person is more offensive. It includes unobstructed facial language, eye-contact, verbal comments, body odors, and greater capacity for violence.

Steadily facing someone with eye contact is rarely accidental. It is usually made to either establish dominance or communication. You can see the dominance component play throughout the animal kingdom. But these two fighting girls are not interested in friendly communication. More of the top girl's front is unobstructed than the bottom girl's.

This dominant front psychologically attacks the bottom girl.

Facial language from the top girl of confidence, smug superiority, and calm demeanor communicate success. The top girl's facial language, eye-contact, and verbal threats have greater impact because of her dominant position.

If the bottom girl shows confidence, makes eye contact, or makes verbal threats, they are not backed with real power. They are laughable and more likely to be dismissed.

If other people are around, the bottom girl is more vulnerable if one of them decides to attack, because then she will have to deal with the top girl *and* this other person. Her head could be easily stomped on by a bystander. A friend of the top girl could easily help keep the bottom girl pinned so that the top girl has more freedom to land punches, pull hair, scratch eyes, poke eyes, choke, or create other major damage in a very short amount of time.

But a friend of the bottom girl would first have to unseat the top girl, and then pin her down before she could be attacked as effectively. By this time, a comrade of the top girl could intervene to even the odds.

3 PSYCHOLOGICAL ADVANTAGES

We all possess a personal bubble of space around us. Because it is invisible, the boundaries of this owned area can often be disputed.

Our senses help delineate this invisible space, especially sight, touch, and smell.

You can observe the effects of this bubble at a gym. One person's strong body odor may cause others to move on to more distant machines. Or if others are attracted to the person, they may desire to be closer to this person's space.

A person often stands by the weights that he is using, having them within or nearby to his personal bubble. This helps communicate to others that the weights are his for the time being.

As you enter a stranger's bubble, you may become aware of his scent. You will probably feel uncomfortable from being so close to his body. If he makes a comment such as, "I'm using those weights," his words are more impactful psychologically from his scent and body already having claimed ownership over the space.

Not to be crude, but simply to elucidate the point—if you fart, you can watch people move away as you have unfairly expanded your personal bubble and colored it with a toxic smell.

The senses of sight and touch also help define this bubble. Stand an inch away from another person and observe what happens. Most likely, she will feel uncomfortable by the sight of your physical invasion. She observes you almost touching her. She sees your face too close to her own. She feels your breaths on her skin. She will either move away or try to get you to move.

However, if you observe a couple in a good relationship, they can be very close. This is because of an agreed upon, mutual type of ownership of each other. "You are my lover, and I am yours." A shared space exists between them.

The top girl forced her adversary inside the bubble that she owns. As such, her adversary is in her territory. Most things here have been and are her possessions: her body, hair, smell, clothing, watches, bracelets, purses, phone, jewelry, etc. Even people who get this close to her are perceived with a type of ownership: *her* best friend or *her* boyfriend.

Being forced into her domain suggests the bottom girl being owned as well.

A visceral attitude of *you are in my place* leaks out

from the top girl.

To compound this, the top girl has simultaneously invaded the bottom girl's personal space, making it not so personal anymore. Because the bottom girl didn't initiate and cannot change this, the top girl's dominance is validated. She now occupies the bottom girl's space. *Your space is mine* is the attitude from the top girl.

Not only that, she occupies the bottom girl's most prized possession in this space—her very body.

It is like taking possession of something valuable that the bottom girl owns, such as taking her car without her permission.

Another space invasion dynamic can be seen before a fight when one girl gets into the other's face. She does this by standing so close to the other that their faces almost touch. If not as an attempt to show dominance, then please explain this action.

The personal bubble can also be observed from common exclamations, such as, "This is my spot in the line," "I'm standing here," "Don't touch me," "Back off!" and even feeling righteous about pushing other people away if they get too close.

But the bottom girl cannot push the top one away. She cannot stop the other from literally touching her body.

Imagine going to a nightclub and watching an attractive woman get as close to your boyfriend as possible, touching him and staying in that position. How would that make you feel? You would probably try to put a stop to this as soon as possible. If personal space has nothing to do with ownership, then why wouldn't you allow this to occur? What difference would standing five feet from him or one inch from him mean?

What does it mean at a nightclub when a strange undesired man places his hand on your buttocks? Why do you feel righteous about slapping him or pushing him away?

Although he may be trying, he does not own that part of your body.

Why do we tell our children not to get into the personal space of a strange adult's car? The answer is they may be owned by the larger stranger, meaning the stranger will have dominant control of them.

Being lower than your opponent is a psychological inferior position.

Imagine looking up at an angry person about three feet taller than yourself. So if your height was five feet, four inches, then you would be looking up at someone eight feet, four inches. That is what the bottom girl is essentially doing. She is looking up at an enraged head which looms three feet over hers.

And the crowd of people standing around is much higher than herself. This can be quite intimidating, given that some people may be unfriendly and aggressive.

Imagine lying on the sidewalk in a large city during a busy time for foot traffic. You could get accidently trampled upon. Your instinct would be to stand up immediately.

Lying on the ground is a vulnerable position.

Higher is a more strategic position.

Predators often seek elevated ground to gain advantage. You rarely see a lion or cat seek a lower place to start a fight (unless it offers the power of concealment). They even leap up or lift themselves on their hind legs during a fight to increase their threat. They prefer higher ground, even trees, when real danger is around. Higher is identified as safer.

Many animals—for example, bears, gorillas, and sea lions—raise themselves off the ground to appear taller, larger, and more threatening to their opponent.

When do you see a bear lay on its back to prepare for an attack? Never. When do you see a dog do this? A dog only takes this position when it feels safe or submissive.

The fact that the top girl forced the other to the ground is a primal psychological boost for her. The bottom girl's position is instinctually weaker *and* submissive. Both girls necessarily feel this.

We sit on a tree branch, a floating log, or a raft to remain *above* waters which may contain dangerous predators, coldness, or potential drowning. Even if you know how to swim, you must stick your head *above* the water frequently to intake air to keep yourself alive.

This instinct of being above something to stay alive or safe is a potent psychological force.

After a fight, it is not uncommon for the bottom

person to stay on the ground to show that she is submissive, has given up, is no longer a threat, and no longer desires to fight. Sometimes the standing opponent will even tell the supine girl not to get up, or she will be beaten down again.

People who are sick, tired, or injured lie down. It *is* the weaker position.

Just in regards to physics, if you are higher than another object and are as massive, you have a greater potential energy. You can stomp, jump or drop onto the other person, using your body weight as a weapon that pummels into them. And of course you can pin them down.

Royalty, dictators, and other people in positions of power have historically resided on higher seats to psychologically accentuate their position.

A prince or princess is called "your *High*ness."

People kneel in prayer, lowering themselves on purpose to show respect and submissiveness to a god. Some people bow to others as a sign of respect or that they are not a threat. The bottom girl has been forced into this lower position.

Just in regards to words, synonyms for surrender include *bow, buckle, cave, go down, go under, and submit.* And words are powerful. They are how we think.

We tell our boss, "I'm on top of it," "I got it under control," "I'm on it," to explain our power over the situation.

Many animals hold their head high and raise their tails to appear dominant and more threatening. A lowering of the head is usually submissive.

The top girl literally looks down at the bottom girl's low head. She may even position her head directly over the bottom girl's head. And the bottom girl looks up to the top girl.

These arrangements mirror certain attitudes in our society. One is of looking up to people we respect, admire, and want to follow. The other is of looking down at those people we don't respect, don't admire, and are seen as unworthy and lower than ourselves.

Think of the phrases people use such as, "You are beneath me," "I am taking the high road," "I would like to rise to her morals," and "I am above that," as potential examples.

On top often means "better than." Our society has these types of long held beliefs driven into us throughout our lives. A top student with the highest grades, listed higher than others; a top team of the NBA with the highest record of wins; the best basketball player with the highest number of baskets; a top scientist better than all others; a quarterback player above the rest; being an Olympian gold medalist and standing on the highest platform when receiving the gold medal; on top of the world; on top of your job—all these portray that being above, higher than, or on top of others is better.

And *below* means "less than." You scored below average on the test; you are on the bottom of the list; your wins in baseball is below everyone else's wins; your successful work with clients is too low to keep you employed; your intelligence is the lowest; you won the least amount of games in the tournament—all are further examples of this.

The hand gesture of *thumbs up* has a positive meaning versus *thumbs down* which has a negative meaning.

Even God and heaven are pictured above, and Satin and hell are pictured below in literary references and works of art.

The aggregation of all these attitudes cannot help but leak out when one girl sits atop another.

People raise their heads and hands high when victorious, sometimes jumping in the air for a greater effect. Sport teammates often raise the best player of the game on their shoulders to celebrate his or her greatness and dominance. Cheerleaders throw another member of their squad high into the air to raise the emotions of the crowd.

The top girl is already in this higher position.

She is identified as the winner. She may even do a little "winning dance" (more common in play fights), with her arms waving and her body jiggling on the bottom girl, accentuating the bottom girl's defeat and adding a tease of humiliation.

There are entrenched beliefs in our society of winners being superior to losers, at least in the competition that was won. The label of loser is a psychological hit to the bottom girl. This nurtures her enemy's confidence and decays hers.

We usually sit on things that are relatively

unimportant (chairs, benches, couches, pillows, bikes, toilets). In fact, their only value is for our *use*. They exist to provide rest, support, comfort, transportation, or disposal of our waste.

As such, the bottom girl is in that same position of being used. She is taking the place of a mere object—something of low value. This is dehumanizing to her.

The bottom girl's desires and feelings do not matter to her enemy. She is being treated without such human components, and is at the will of her enemy.

The person sitting is important, not the seat.

We are meant to sit in a seat for possibly hours at a time.

In fact, we often forget about our seats and focus on more important things, such as homework, a conversation, eating, driving, painting, watching television, surfing the internet, reading a book, etc.

The bottom girl's function now is to support her enemy's weight and provide her enemy with rest. This has been forced onto her. As she comes to this realization, she becomes demoralized.

Compared to a wooden chair, plastic chair, hard floor, or cement bench, she is a comfortable seat. Her body feels soft and spongy. Even if the top girl sits on her adversary's rib cage, she is provided a seat with gentle give.

It is rare and brief when we sit on another human being. When it occurs, it cannot be isolated from the many thousands of hours of sitting on unimportant things.

Just count the number of hours you are sitting on objects in just one day. Then multiply that by 365, and then multiply that number by your age. If you are eighteen years old, this number is probably around 100,000 hours. This enormous history of our seats being less important than ourselves exacerbates the sense inferiority of the bottom girl.

The top girl's anus and genitals—where solid and liquid wastes are excreted—rest on the bottom girl. Just because this is so disgusting that it is either denied or never publicly discussed does not reduce its profound psychological impact.

Besides being worthless, human waste is repulsive, disgusting, stinky, dirty, contaminated with germs dangerous to us, and to be avoided *at all costs*.

The gases from the bowels contain one of the most lethal gases: hydrogen sulfide, which is also flammable. Urine outside of the body releases the intense smell of ammonia.

Our own excrement is repulsive to us, but an enemy's is exponentially worse. Yet the bottom girl is not merely forced near these orifices of her adversary, but is in contact with them, apart from one to two layers of clothing.

They are pressing against her body. She can feel their warmth.

It humiliates her to the extreme. There exist few situations more humiliating.

The top girl used the toilet probably several times

in the previous eight hours, giving her the fresh mental association of the other girl in that same position: *there to receive waste*. This dynamic becomes even more intense if she had defecated or urinated just minutes before the fight; or if she is currently menstruating.

If this association is not consciously done, it will be unconsciously achieved, with similar psychological impacts.

The bottom girl also makes this humiliating and degrading association as she observes, feels, and possibly smells her enemy's areas of waste discharge. This drives her to feel inferior and owned.

She has been forced to remain in perhaps the most unwanted area. It unequivocally displays her enemy's rule over her.

A subconscious or conscious fear may develop within her of being defeated, bled, or urinated on.

After all, it would be the ultimate humiliation for her. What if the top girl has diarrhea? The danger of a little coming out could be real. What if her menstruation cycle is irregular or a little off, and she is bleeding that day? What if the top girl has a full bladder? A little might come out. She might even be one of those girls who has poor bladder control.

Because of the awkward position of the bottom girl underneath her enemy's private parts, onlookers sometimes yell, "That looks so wrong!"

Think of the verbal attack, "Kiss my ass." Why do people say this? They don't say, "Kiss my eye," to hurt you. They don't say, "Kiss my shoulder." They say, "Kiss my ass."

This is especially visceral due to the place of the body they are ordering the other to kiss. This is a most objectionable place for an enemy. It is a prime dirty spot. The comment attempts to gain power through degradation and humiliation of the other person.

But to truly place your ass on your adversary is not merely words, but reality. It is an intense demonstration of power.

A similar type of ownership through humiliation is exemplified in play fights when the top girl stuffs a dirty sock into the face of the bottom victim.

The top girl has not just forced her adversary into her personal bubble of space, but also into her *private* personal space.

This is very different from other parts of her body. (Notice how we offer our hands to strangers as a form of greeting, but never our bottoms. Why is that?)

This space contains the top girl's private parts, which she has totally owned and has been her exclusive area for all of her life. This space is so much hers that no one else has been allowed to see it, touch it, smell it, taste it, or be within close proximity of it without her permission. She is the exclusive person who has the freedom to do these things. She is the total ruler over this domain.

This space is where very private actions occur on a

regular basis. This is where she defecates, urinates, farts, sheds dead tissue and bleeds, sweats to a greater degree, cultivates a high degree of bacteria, stinks, creates smegma, cleaning fluids, and fluids of lubrication, becomes sexually aroused, masturbates, orgasms and ejaculates. This is her innermost sanctum.

This is where she can give birth to life that she will identify as hers.

She has now forced her adversary into her completely *owned* territory. This cannot help but also convey stronger ownership over her adversary.

In fact, it is not uncommon to display banners at a high school or college sport game with a message similar or identical to, "This is our house." This message is an attempt to mark territory, and convey ownership and dominance over the opposing team.

Knowing that her private space contains her enemy lifts the top girl's confidence because it is her "house," or owned area.

Tonight, if you dig into the soil on your land and find a gold coin, wouldn't you believe you have rights to it because it was within your private property?

One of the definitions of *private* is belonging to some particular person.

The top girl's private space is also charged with private emotions, increasing entitlement of the area.

Sensitive and emotional body parts of the top girl are fixed on the bottom girl. The genital area produces sexual feelings—perhaps the most private and personal of emotions—which the top girl identifies as intimately hers, which she no doubt owns because they *are her feelings*. These are intensely personal of which no one else feels but her.

The anus is similar with regards to powerful feelings, which occur during bowel movements or anal sex. Some people report great pleasure or orgasmic-like feelings during these activities. This may help explain the use of anal beads or fingering the anus during sexual activity.

Urination shivers or Post-Micturition Convulsion Syndrome also occur from this private area of the body.

The bottom girl is caged in enemy territory where her enemy's exclusively owned, intimate, intense feelings originate. This territory also contains intensely owned physical parts of this hated person. She feels inundated by her enemy.

Everything intimate of this person she detests has been pushed onto her.

Our bottoms are not simply another part of our body, but also very strong olfactory places.

In the ages when our ancestors didn't have shavers for hair in the pubic and anus regions, showers, running water, soap, toilet paper, wet wipes, tampons or pads, and clothing—their scents, urine, blood, and feces were much more readily deposited onto the places they sat. This conveyed an aftereffect of ownership of those places, somewhat like leaving your jacket on a seat does nowadays.

To help understand this concept, imagine if a stinky stranger sat on your pillow. You would abandon it for another due to the stranger's strong odor still emanating and claiming ownership over it. You would not want to put your head where that foul scent continues to reside.

Some people are even leery to sit in a chair that a homeless person who hadn't showered for weeks just vacated.

Perhaps you have a memory of a very hot day in which you were discomforted by another person's strong body odor who sat close to you.

Do you remember the time when you entered a bathroom stall and smelled the worst smell of your life? It didn't feel like your space, did it? You wanted to get out of there as fast as possible, right? Someone else occupied that stall before you, and she could come back and have easy access to it again because everyone else abandons it for more congenial smelling stalls.

This long history of our worst stenches being deposited on our seats, comforted by our own smells and discomforted by strangers' smells, has added to a psychological component of owning our seats. (More on this in the chapter of sensual dynamics.)

Apart from smell, a person relates ownership to anything she sits on. This is so ordinary and is done so frequently that people forget its significance until someone sits on another person.

Everything the top girl sat on for every second of

every hour during her life was hers as she sat on it. *This is my chair now because I'm sitting on it. This is my spot on the couch. This is my spot on the beach because I'm sitting here. I'm on this swing, so go find your own swing. This is my turn on the inflatable raft in the pool; I'm using it. This is my seat in the movie theater. This is my turn on the ride, so wait until I'm done. I'm sitting on the bike right now because it is my turn, so I get to use it until I'm done. This is my seat in the classroom because I've sat here all year long. I'm on this yoga mat, so go get your own. This is my office chair that I sit in every day.* All of these are pervasive norms and attitudes she has adopted and experienced throughout her life. These are so entrenched and powerful that other people almost always move on to different spots that are not taken.

Try it out. Go to a movie theater, a park, a coffeehouse, or a library and have a seat.

Watch how many people walk by you to find another seat that they can claim. Every single person out of hundreds who passes by you identifies the seat as yours.

People do not even question your ownership of it.

But even in rare circumstances when someone demands your seat, that person would first have to move you to get it. Until then, it is yours, being *used* by you.

Now consider the effect of the top girl sitting on the other girl.

While the top girl sits on the other, this attitude of ownership translates not only to both girls, but also to bystanders. She is occupying the seat. No one else is or can at the moment.

The top girl may say things like, "You're mine, bitch."

The crowd may yell, "She's your bitch," or "You own her." Or they may yell to the bottom girl, "You got owned!"

If you are still in doubt that sitting equals owning, you are pretty stubborn indeed, but go back to the coffee shop, library, or class.

Now try to get someone to move who is already sitting.

Go ahead, what's stopping you? Societal norms? What norms? Just tell them to move. After all, they don't own that spot, do they?

A frequent reply will be something like, "No, I'm sitting here right now. Go find your own seat."

Back to the two girls fighting, who is doing the sitting? Psychologically, who owns that seat?

As a child, the top girl learned that when she sits on a small toy, book, or other object, it helps her keep ownership over it. Teachers and other adults were less likely to reach for it because it was hidden or underneath her private parts. Other children had more difficulty obtaining it, either because it was hidden or because they had to move her first to get to it. Due to her weight being on it, her position was the strongest way to hold onto it.

The bottom girl also learned these things as a child.

Picture another situation in which a family is visiting a hotel room with several beds within it. Perhaps you have seen a movie or had a personal experience like this. How did one of the children claim a bed they wanted? A common method is to run to the bed and *sit* on it, saying, "This one is mine!" concretely claiming ownership by putting herself on it and something else she owns such as her suitcase or jacket.

Or recall how children claim seats in the car. They rush inside and sit on the seat they want, saying, "I got here first!"

We even make games in our society demonstrating this type of ownership.

Recall the classic game of musical chairs. It is when a group of people walk around a circle of chairs while music is playing. There is one chair less than the number of people in the group. When the music stops, everyone attempts to gain possession of a chair by being the first to sit on it. The people who get seated have earned the chair and are safe. The standing people remaining must rush to find another seat to occupy. The last person standing is eliminated from the game and takes a chair with them so that on the next turn someone else will be eliminated. These turns continue until the person who acquires possession of the last seat is the winner.

The above conditions and many more like them create a consistent, expansive understanding that sitting equals owning.

Now go back to the top girl sitting on her enemy and imagine her thoughts.

Imagine the bottom girl's thoughts of being sat on.

If you still doubt that sitting on someone creates a temporary ownership of her, picture going to the park on a Saturday afternoon, find someone who is relaxing on the grass, and sit on her. What do you think would happen next?

What would she say or do? Why?

Even though she was already desiring to rest on the grass for a while, chances are she will immediately begin communicating or struggling to reestablish the freedom and the ability to move whenever *she* so chooses, not when you choose for her.

So what is freedom to move your body? In part, it is ownership of your body.

Quadriplegic people who used to have complete control of their bodies have to mourn this loss of freedom and mastery of their bodies. They have to deal with the feelings of decreased ownership of their bodies. A common feeling is a loss of self. They cannot command their legs and arms as they once could. Eventually, they can come to an acceptance and sense of ownership once again, but this takes months, if not years to accomplish.

Definitions of ownership include to have power or mastery over something; to have or hold as property; or belonging to oneself.

Going back to the girl at the park, besides immobility, she has the additional dynamic of someone on top of her body.

People even claim ownership of places that their car is on top of. These places can be a rare parking space at a crowded mall or a position in line at a drive-through restaurant. Similar to the personal space of your body, a car has a personal bubble surrounding it. When someone tailgates you, it brings feelings of encroachment into your space. Or you may tailgate someone to show dominance to try to get them to move faster.

Even a mountain is not considered conquered until you climb and stand or sit on the top of it.

Hunters frequently put their foot on top of a deer after they've killed it, showing dominance, ownership, and conquering. Wrestlers sometimes do this to their opponent, calling it a victory pose.

People may leave their sweater or their jacket on top of a seat to show other people that the seat has been claimed already.

A person at the laundry mat will quickly begin putting her clothes in a cart or machine to claim temporary ownership of it so she can use it at her leisure.

Countries put their flags—something personal to that country—on new land they claim. The United States put a flag on the moon to show dominance in space travel, if not to claim that spot on the moon.

Israelites exercise ownership of particular religious land by continuing to reside *on* it, despite protests from Palestinians.

How many more examples do I need to give?

Why would we exercise all these claims of ownership unless they truly had meaning and power to others?

Even animals understand that they own what they are on top of.

For example, a dog lies on, sits on, and jumps on things sometimes simply to claim them as his territory. These can be people, other dogs, couches, bones, or whatever. It doesn't matter. What is important is that it is ownership.

Try moving a dog off the couch. He will likely resist you in some way, unless he is very well behaved (submissive to the alpha—master). He might feel entitled enough to growl or snap at you because he has claimed this as his spot on the couch.

A lioness positions arm and paw over, body close to, and head over her prey not simply to make it easy to eat, but also to claim ownership over the food so unfamiliar animals don't try to steal some. The powerful parts of the lion—teeth and mouth and claws—are over the meal, exercising greater ownership.

This ownership explains why some dominate dogs feel entitled to growl and snap at you if you invade their space during meal time. Their greatest powers are directly over the food—their teeth and mouth.

Notice they do not exercise this type of dominate behavior before they are positioned over the food, when you are preparing it at the kitchen counter. At these times, you are closest to the food. The dogs see you as claiming ownership over it.

Like a dog's teeth and mouth, the powerful parts of the top girl are over the bottom girl. This includes the obvious, her fists which can punch. But it also includes her body.

The female body is equipped with its own special powers, as opposed to a male body which has its own. Females have the miraculous power to nurture a fetus in their uterus and to give birth to human life.

This is an immense power and can change the lives of many people.

In addition, the female body as an attractive force is a fierce influence in our society. Advertisers use a beautiful model and her sexuality to help sell their product, and it really does work. This is not to say that males don't also have physical sexual power, but that women have more. Research income levels of female top models verses male top models. Research how much female pornography makes compared to male pornography. Research numbers and income levels of female verses male strippers. A woman's body is more idolized by both sexes than a man's body alone is idolized by both sexes.

(An attractive male body when coupled with high social or financial success equalizes this unbalanced dynamic. But there just aren't as many of these types of men as there are attractive females, so women are in greater competition with one another for these alpha mates.)

The female gender dominates beauty contests. Please find the most reasonable rationale for this.

Simply women's clothing alone demonstrates a greater showing off of their bodies as a power of attraction: exposed midriffs, tight jeans, form fitting leggings, skirts, mini-skirts, short shorts, short dresses, strappy shoes exposing toes and other parts of the feet, off the shoulder tops, low cut blouses, tiny bikinis, G-string underwear, laced lingerie, see-through lingerie, etcetera. This is so much a part of our culture that it may be hard to recognize.

This power of physical beauty is frequently used outside of the fight to influence social status amongst girls, and used in competitiveness with other girls for a guy.

Although the top girl cannot use her powers of beauty and birth in a physical manner in the fight, they have some psychological impact simply by existing *on top of* her adversary.

If she had a weapon in her hand, this threat would increase her power, even if she never used it. Simply having it within her grasp would likely increase her enemy's submission.

The top girl's powers of beauty and birth are not absent of threat. She may use them after the fight to win over a guy that the bottom girl likes, become pregnant with his baby, or influence a group of girlfriends to ostracize the bottom girl.

The top girl's beauty can also be comparable to a weapon by likely increasing the number of people who observe her enemy's submission and humiliation. This can occur through attracting a larger crowd during the fight and/or a greater number of views afterwards of the uploaded videos on the Internet.

The bottom girl's beauty actually works against her because this also is likely to increase the amount of people who view her in a weak and dominated state.

Back to the subject of sitting equals owning, if the top girl scoots up close to the other's face, this increases ownership of it.

She has brought her personal space that is her domain to this face. Her knees, thighs, calves, feet, and pelvis besiege it; her body looms over it; her head hovers high above it; her private parts crowd it, and her most intimate scents invade it. Her enemy's face is now truly submerged in her territory. Her entire body lays claim over it, including areas of intimate power.

This move towards the enemy's head is not infrequent in girl fights. The top girl can most easily disable her enemy's arms by sliding forward and pinning them with her shins and thighs. In the heat of battle, it comes more naturally to gain this advantage, despite any social taboo of this position.

She has greater control of her enemy's body and arms. She can hurt her enemy at will.

She truly owns that countenance that inflicted so much suffering on her in the past. The face that had previously smirked, glared, laughed, jeered at her, shown confidence and dominance, made verbal put-downs, spread lies, looked smug, and teased her—now belongs to the top girl.

The source of all thoughts, actions, and utterances that had hurt the top girl is below her. The head. If her adversary had stolen her boyfriend, she finally gains a sense of control over this betrayal. She created a space where she has power over the past treachery of the other girl.

These sudden, severe powers are intoxicating for the top girl. Her enemy's face shows fear, embarrassment, humiliation, and a lack of confidence—all of which she created.

Besides that, she is seated on her enemy's chest.

Given our discussion so far, you could probably guess what this entails.

Directly underneath her is her adversary's heart. This is what gives the bottom girl life. It is the central part of her, which is why it is called the heart. It also is symbolically the place where her feelings reside. The top girl actually feels her enemy's fear through speeding heartbeats against her crotch. She feels her enemy's breaths lifting her body. While she sits, she claims these as hers. She owns the bottom girl's life force and, in a metaphorical sense, owns the bottom girl's intimate feelings.

Not only that, but she also sits on one of the bottom girl's private areas (her breasts), gaining ownership over this very personal space that no one else has been allowed to touch, let alone sit on.

This area can also be sensitive at times. And with

the weight of her enemy on it, it may become painful.

All these influences combine to create a profound position for the top girl.

In addition, all she has to do is raise herself onto her knees and her crotch and body will be directly above opponent's head—another type of ownership.

This will likely occur when she decides to get off her enemy.

Sitting is a more permanent position than standing or walking. We sit down on something to rest, relax, and *stay for a while*. This conveys a stronger ownership of a spot on a rock, a couch, a chair, or another place than standing. We have staked out our seat and intend to stay until rested and satisfied.

Standing is more transitory, for all one has to do is begin walking to move away. But if one is sitting, she must first get up before she can walk away. It is a little like parking your car and removing the key versus idling the car in gear. The top girl has parked herself on the other girl.

To compound this, the bottom girl lies on her back, which is even a more permanent and disabling position than sitting.

When a person lies down, they must first sit up, then stand in order to walk away. A person sitting merely needs to stand. Lying down is associated with sleeping or greater rest than simply sitting. People who are dead and who are put to rest almost always are lying down. When we sleep at night for eight hours, we are lying down. It is a greater and more enduring position of rest. And, as such, it is a more difficult position to get out of than sitting.

This means that the bottom girl is more fixed in her position of vulnerability, subjugation, and submission. Alternatively this means that the top girl exercises more dominance, control, and power, even if she wasn't sitting atop the supine girl. But since she is, this exacerbates her power.

Also, your personal bubble of space is fixed in one spot when you sit. If you are walking, it is constantly changing. This means that you are not claiming any spot as your own. When you sit, your bubble remains fixed on an area and so also claims temporary ownership over that place.

People also claim possession over seats they have vacated for a short while. *That was my spot on the couch; I was sitting there; I was using the hammock, and I just got up to get something to eat; I was riding that bike; I'm still using that stool*—all are more norms and attitudes we have adopted and experienced to claim rights over a seat. The seat may even still be warm from our body heat. It may still possess our scent. These lingering signs of ourselves on the seat help us continue to claim ownership.

Since the top girl sits on the bottom girl, this impacts both of them even after the top girl gets up.

The longer the top girl holds her seat on the bottom girl, the more impact the message has of dominance and ownership. The more time we possess anything in our society, the more likely others will believe we own it. The passage of time shows that no one else has claimed it, no one else wants or has the power to take it, and that we can keep possession of it. And people come to assume it is ours, even if it is not.

In the circumstance of one girl pinning another, as each minute passes, it is greater understood that the girl on top is keeping the other under her control. The longer she sits, the clearer the message is that she is forcing her adversary to remain in an uncomfortable, humiliating, submissive, and repulsive position. Each passing minute gives the bottom girl more time and opportunity to free herself. But with the growing empirical evidence that she cannot, the belief of the top girl's dominance strengthens.

A longer pin also demonstrates the top girl's commitment and perseverance to stay in control. Each passing minutes offers her many opportunities to get up and leave. But as she stays seated, she demonstrates her frightening resolve to remain dominant and to further harm the bottom girl.

The top girl wins more than just ownership; her enemy loses self-possession, increasing the top girl's victory.

For the girl on the bottom, she has lost control of her body movement. This loss of control, over time, fortifies the sensation that she no longer owns or has mastery over her body, but that the other girl does. This loss is tremendous because she has possessed her body all the rest of her waking life. But now, her enemy owns it.

This dynamic can be observed in sensory deprivation chambers. We lose the ability to use our senses, giving us the feeling that we are out of or separate from our bodies. In other words, we lose ownership of our bodies for a brief time.

Her enemy owning her movement is a powerful lack of self-possession. Do not underestimate the importance of movement. The bottom girl must *move* to take basic care for herself—to breathe freely, eat, and drink. She can't use the restroom if she needs to; she can't scratch an itch, can't comfort herself by shifting into a better position, read a required book for school, play a game, visit her friends, meet appointments and deadlines, use her phone, or get any goals accomplished throughout the day. The top girl can leave whenever she wants. The bottom girl cannot.

Her enemy's body suddenly gains a higher degree of meaning in her life because it can and does inflict physical and psychological distress in the moment. The top girl's fists mean more. Her feet mean more. Her calves mean more. Her thighs, weight, and crotch mean more. They all become important to the bottom girl because they confine and hurt her. The top girl knows this at some level, and it raises her sense of importance as a person.

The top girl has a gain of self, gaining power over something that was previously out of her control. Her adversary had hurt her, and now she has control over this influence, broadening the scope of herself.

Things have finally changed. Feeling powerless is no longer an issue. She feels relief.

Her position on top of her enemy is intoxicating. It plays a part for some girls to use fighting to resolve conflicts again, especially if they have not healed from past physical or emotional abuse.

The girl on top sees weakness in the other girl's face. She can finally challenge her enemy's social supremacy with physical supremacy.

While in this dominant position, she can bring up a topic that other girl was previously confident in to squash it.

"Mark is my man! Stay away from him."

Girls have a larger vocabulary and verbally communicate more than guys before adulthood (some argue this even during adulthood in regards to relationships). Communication is very important to girls, especially in regards to relationships.

From her position of sitting on her enemy, the top girl gains power in communicating.

When you are in a vulnerable position such as the bottom girl, it is more difficult to disobey those who are more powerful.

Think of situations at your job in which your boss tells you something and how importantly you treat those words. Your livelihood may be on the line, so you listen more intently. You tend not to argue with the boss. You tend to obey the boss. You tend to feel submissive to the boss.

Also, for the top girl, it is different than before the fight. Her communication cannot be physically retaliated against as it could before pinning her rival. Now the bottom girl is more likely to passively listen and has much more difficulty using violence if angered. So the top girl is safer to verbally express herself.

The exact opposite is true for the bottom girl. If the bottom girl expresses something offensive, then her rival can easily commit physical violence upon her. So she is less safe in expressing herself.

Also, in regards to conversation, the bottom girl cannot think as clearly as her rival due to having greater levels of fear, reducing the higher functioning of her brain. The conversation is thus more one-sided, in favor of her enemy.

All these factors combine to help the top girl win an argument more easily.

"Why were you talking shit about me?" she may confidently confront her rival. "I saw you at Jessica's house hanging out with Britney. She told me you were telling people that I thought I was better than everyone else."

The bottom girl will have more difficulty forming an intelligent, reasonable argument of defense.

In regards to physicality, simply taking the breaths necessary for speech will be more difficult because of the weight on her lungs or stomach.

The top girl also has gained a captive audience with her rival. It is not just physical immobility that the bottom girl endures. She is forced to pay attention to her enemy; whereas before the fight, she may have been ignoring the other girl for months.

The top girl forces the bottom girl to notice her, to validate that she is real, to validate that her feelings of anger matter. They matter if only because they hurt the bottom girl now.

These powers are very alluring to the top girl because she often felt unheard or not important enough by the bottom girl, her words not taken seriously.

The top girl is now able to say whatever she had wanted and knows she will be heard. She is more important now to her enemy. The conversation can last as long as she wants. She is finally able to command her adversary's attention to her old feelings. Her adversary cannot run, cannot walk away, and cannot pretend she doesn't exist. She can sit there until she is heard.

And her adversary is forced to face her when she is most strong.

Guys in the crowd may yell, "Don't just sit there and talk, hit her!" not understanding the greater role of conversation in female relationships.

She fills her enemy's vision. Her smell is saturating her enemy's nostrils. Her voice is loud as she hunches over to yell into the other's face.

She may exclaim, "You spread lies that I'm a slut!" The bottom girl will have more difficulty denying this now.

The top girl can get into her adversary's face as much as she wants, as close as she wants, whenever she wants.

The bottom girl becomes discouraged that she cannot move away while her personal space is being invaded by the loud, hurtful volume to her ears with her adversary's verbal assaults.

The top girl may taunt her enemy to try to get up to prove to everyone that her enemy is truly powerless. This helps defeat the bottom girl's resolve. This moves her to submission.

The top girl may tease, "Is that all you got?" "Look at you now," or "What're you going to do?" to help cement her opponent's powerlessness and weakness.

She may ask sarcastically, "You like that?" to bring her opponent to answer, "No." This highlights her power of making her opponent suffer unpleasant things.

"Do you want more?" may be a question to promote the bottom girl to say, "No," and to submit. She may ask, "Are you done?" to prompt her enemy to say, "Yes," and to submit.

She may ask, "Does that hurt?" to demonstrate her rule over her enemy's feelings.

The bottom girl may even be forced to do or say things that her opponent wants, much like a slave, puppet, or prisoner. This demonstrates her lack of control. It also makes the top girl feel better from exercising so much influence. She may force her adversary to say, "Uncle," "I surrender," or "I give," in less threatening situations such as a play fight. Or in more threatening situations, she may coerce the girl to beg for her life or say hurtful things about herself such as, "I'm a slut" or "I'm trash."

The girl may be forced to do something humiliating like eat grass, pick her nose, eat boogers, or slap herself. Although these actions might sound silly, they demonstrate the top girl's strength over the other.

The bottom girl is now merely a toy of her enemy.

Friends in the crowd may yell to the top girl, "Get her, Jenna!" as though the bottom girl were simply an object to possess.

The top girl's laughter shows her lack of caring for her enemy's feelings. It communicates that she enjoys her enemy's pain and discomfort.

In her state of confinement, the bottom girl feels a loss of importance. Her feelings have lost the ability to create actions to help her, to respect herself, and to prevent further hurt and loss. Her anger is ineffective to remove loss or hurt; so it just sits inside, having nowhere to go but at herself. This lowers her self-esteem. She becomes angry at herself for being so weak.

It is the top girl's feelings that dictate the next actions, so these escalate in importance to the bottom girl.

Evidence already exists of the top girl's feelings having command—her enemy remains captive on the ground.

She gains a greater sense of self-importance because she is responsible for another person's life. In every moment now, she impacts another person. She is felt by another.

We all have primal fears when trapped underneath things. These may involve being trapped underneath water in which we cannot breathe, being trapped underneath the ground in a confined space with little oxygen, being trapped underneath anything heavy in which we cannot move. One cannot run to safety if one is incapacitated. The bottom girl feels this at a primal level.

And the longer the top girl sits, the more it wears on her opponent. Even though there may be no overt actions by the top girl, *much* is happening.

She is constantly committing covert physical violence.

Her weight rides each of her enemy's breaths. It pressures her enemy's lungs, forcing them to work harder and crowd other vital organs such as the heart.

The bottom girl's breaths become shallower, losing strength to expand normally because of the unnatural load on them. Each fighting inhalation must raise almost all of the top girl's weight, about forty lifts a minute. After just five minutes, this turns into two hundred heavy repetitions.

This weight on the ribcage may also pressure her heartbeats, as demonstrated in CPR compressions.

Her adversary's weight is increasingly identified as

a weapon. This makes the entirety of the girl more threatening. The bottom girl may exclaim, "Get your fat ass off of me!" even if the top girl is not fat. Name calling is simply an attempt to control the other.

As the bottom girl squirms underneath for freedom, she tires. But when she pauses to rest, her lungs continue to labor against the weight, preventing true rest.

Eventually she feels like she can't get enough oxygen and, out of desperation, tries to breathe faster. This paves the way to hyperventilation and a panic attack.

Also, when she stops struggling, her increased heartbeat, breathing, and blood pressure persist in anticipation and defense of further hurt or loss (a state otherwise known as fear). As more time passes, this heightened state becomes more tiresome to endure.

Psychologically, she is constantly being kept in her enemy's private space. This erodes her sense of personal space and diminishes the size of her personal bubble.

Not knowing how long she will be trapped in this tight space, the feeling of claustrophobia grows.

Deep breathing is one way to relax, but she cannot effectively do this.

Any denial she had of her weakened position erodes. She feels to a greater extent her abject vulnerability to her enemy. Questioning how long she can survive like this, she may worry whether she will *ever* be released and whether she may die. In her desperation, she may plead, "Get off me! I can't breathe."

For the duration of the pin, she continually sees, smells, and feels her enemy. She is entrapped in her enemy's dominance. The longer the pin, the more her enemy's strength becomes etched into her mind and the longer she suffers in a state of helplessness.

As time passes, the bottom girl may lose feeling in her arms as her opponent's shins remain dug into the flesh and nerves.

The sustained weight on her ribcage can cause rib cartilage to become inflamed. These are alarming chest pains that can be mistaken for a heart attack.

Swallowing is more difficult when you're lying on your back, and can add to a choking sensation if saliva drips down the esophagus or accidently enters the lungs, causing coughing. Also, if her nose is runny or bleeding, this may drip down as well, causing the same effects.

If she had discomfort from the top girl sitting on her partially full or totally full bladder at the start, this only worsens if the top girl still sits there. And the bladder continues to fill as time passes. She may actually urinate on herself, or at least the fear of urinating on herself surfaces in these circumstances.

If she had eaten recently, her stomach is enlarged with food and will feel uncomfortable with the weight of the top girl bearing down on it for a lengthy time. Acid reflux is also more likely as her enemy's weight and movements increase the pressure on her stomach. This can cause burning pains in the chest, choking from food coming up, nausea and fears of vomiting.

If she has gas, cramps, constipation, nausea, or diarrhea, she may feel exceptional discomfort as her guts are being compressed. With diarrhea, the horror intensifies of potentially defecating on herself in public as she has no means to use the bathroom. With nausea, a similar type of dread applies.

The top girl may make threats such as, "I can sit here all day," further discouraging and demoralizing the bottom girl.

The longer the pin, the more likely the top girl will eventually pass gas (more likely in play fights). This would not only be disgusting for the bottom girl at such close range to her head, but also take up the fresh oxygen that she so values to breathe.

The more time passes, the more the bottom girl is identified as an unimportant object just to sit on. She is increasingly seen as having taken place of a mere chair, an object which we commonly sit on for long periods of time with no concern of the constant pressure we place on it.

It is a way of treating her like trash. Her worth decreases in the direction of a chair's worth as the top girl continually places her in that role, of which she cannot escape.

The longer pins also lead to the bottom girl becoming used to being controlled by her enemy. She becomes accustomed to being inferior to the top girl and giving into the top girl's demands. This can create greater submissiveness as an accumulation of many moments of powerlessness leave a stronger psychological imprint of powerlessness after the fight.

Even the crowd becomes used to seeing the bottom girl as impotent and weak. And the longer she is pinned, the greater the number of people who might gather around or pass by to watch her impotency, increasing her humiliation.

Each passing minute makes both girls acutely aware how much the bottom girl is at her adversary's mercy to be released.

This relentless weight, the difficulty of each breath against it, the inescapable stink of her opponent, the continuous humiliation and debasement, the unending domination, the unremitting loss of freedom, the vulnerability, the worry of the next exploitation and its extent, the growing fear of death, the erosion of energy and spirit, the inability to overcome these conditions—all wear on her.

In contrast, the top girl's relatively relaxed sitting position rejuvenates her.

Her heartbeat and blood pressure decrease as time passes from her safer and more comfortable position. Her fear is reduced.

With each breath, she has no pressure from a hundred-twenty-pound body on her lungs or vital organs like her opponent. Her breathing becomes more relaxed.

Her efforts to keep herself seated expend much

less energy than her opponent's struggles for freedom. Her sustained control and dominance over her rival heightens her confidence.

When the bottom girl stops struggling, the top girl can rest in a *truly* relaxed state. She may sit up straight, indirectly increasing the weight where she sits, making breathing for her opponent even worse. Her relaxed state may be highlighted by her attention to other activities such as straightening her hair, conversing with bystanders, laughing and smiling, resting her hands on her hips, thighs, or knees like she no longer needs them. Additionally, her opponent's lack of struggling nears an acceptance of defeat, which further emboldens her.

Psychologically, she constantly sees and feels her enemy underneath her private space. Over time, like a chair she has sat on for a while, she becomes more accustomed to see it as her spot.

She notices her enemy's breathing becoming more difficult. She feels shallower and faster breaths lifting her body up. She can hear her enemy's lungs cough or wheeze as breaths become labored. As each of these punishing minutes pass, the top girl's satisfaction grows.

Conversation requires breath, so her adversary may become more silent.

She can look down and watch fear, pain, and submissiveness grow on her enemy's face.

She luxuriates in that she is accomplishing two things at once: resting while still hurting her enemy.

She relishes the greater power of using little energy to accomplish this.

And it is a *hidden* way of hurting her adversary without bystanders noticing and preventing it. All she has to do is sit there.

In fact, the crowd may yell, "Do something," "Don't just sit there. Hit her!" or "This isn't a fight." They don't realize that the fight is still continuing even though no overt actions are being taken.

They also don't see that the battle continues to a greater degree on a psychological level now.

One drawback for the top girl may be that her legs might get uncomfortable if the pin lasts longer than twenty or thirty minutes, but this is a small discomfort compared to what the other girl endures. And it is rare that the top girl needs to keep the other girl down that long.

Alternatively, over time, the bottom girl notices her enemy becoming increasingly confident and satisfied, being able to attend to other activities, and being rewarded with more relaxed breathing and demeanor. This creates greater feelings of inferiority and insecurity for her. She may notice that the people watching do not understand the extent of her suffering, and she may call out, "Get her off me!"

The top girl does not just sit on, but also straddles her opponent. This is a more stable position as opposed to simply sitting.

Her legs are spread wider to increase her balance on the bottom girl, making it more difficult to fall left or right. Her feet may be pointed outward for stability as well. She also has several points of contact to the ground—feet, shins, knees, and sometimes hands—increasing stability and making it more difficult to fall forward or backward. This makes her feel more secure.

Her feet or heels may also be squeezing against her opponent's body, holding her on top. Or her feet may be hooked underneath her enemy, creating a firm hold.

Her straddling also works to prevent her opponent's movement not just from above and below, but also from side to side. The bottom girl is essentially caged in.

The top girl has had command over things she straddled in the past.

She has had frequent experiences of straddling objects to increase her control and improve her balance, such as with bikes, horses, motorcycles, mopeds, jet-skis, surfboards, tree branches when climbing as a child, hoppity-hop toys, merry-go-round animal rides, etc. The straddle position makes it easier for her to ride her opponent with control because her body, legs, and feet work together to keep her on top. Both girls intuitively know this, affecting their confidence levels.

The top girl's legs are either resting on or are very close to the other's arms. Her calves are bigger than her opponent's forearms, and her thighs are gigantic in comparison. Their muscle mass incredibly overpowers those of her opponent's arms.

Not only is this a visual blow, but a physical one as well. Legs are simply stronger than arms. Even if the legs are not pinning the opponent's arms down, within seconds they could. This evokes defeat and weakness within the bottom girl.

As children, both girls came to learn that objects they grasped, they could temporarily own until an adult pried it out of their fingers. But with the top girl's weight, legs, feet, and hands working together, she grasps her opponent much more effectively than with hands alone. Her complex and firmer hold on her adversary yields a stronger sense of possession of this girl.

The top girl can grab hold of her opponent's arms, neck, or hair to help glue her down onto the other girl. With these additional holds, she can pull herself back onto her opponent if she loses balance, is thrown in one direction, or is pushed. These holds act much like a horse's reins, the horn on a Western saddle, a horse's mane, or the rope-hold in a bull ride, providing extra security and stability.

The top girl rides the other girl as she struggles for freedom. The top girl may even accentuate this by bouncing and yelling, "Giddy-up!" (more likely in play fighting). It emphasizes her control over the bottom girl.

The definition of riding something itself is one of power: to sit and travel on the back of an animal that one directs, to be supported, sustained, or conveyed, to sit on and control so as to be carried along, to harass with persistent carping or criticism, to dominate or tyrannize over.

The top girl does not ride to a destination of a place, but rather the destination of conquering the bottom girl's strength and spirit.

Both girls have had thousands of experiences throughout their life of being in control of what they rode. Be it a bicycle, rocking horse, swing, moped, or car, she had control over it. These understandings of her position granting power again infer superiority to her.

And, in contrast, being ridden implies loss of control and inferiority to the rider. It is the bottom girl who is being worked, expending more energy, supporting the other girl's weight, being used and controlled, and will be worn out in the end. She is carrying her enemy to victory.

She is kept on an inferior place—the ground.

This is low, dirty, lacking value, as exemplified by people throwing trash, dumping used liquids and food, spitting, walking, and even sometimes urinating and vomiting on it. Cats, dogs, and birds defecate and urinate on it frequently. Bugs crawl on it. Life dies, decays, and rots on it.

Children often exemplify this worse or unsafe place when they play a game of the floor being hot lava which is to be avoided by touch.

People trample on the smaller life that grows there with mostly disregard, such as grasses, weeds, worms, and bugs.

The bottom girl's hair is collecting dirt, mud, leaves, insects or worse materials from the ground that are unclean or possibly dangerous.

We wipe our feet on doormats before entering a house. Sometimes we even take off our shoes to keep the house really clean.

We often place towels or blankets on the ground before we sit to protect us from its uncleanliness. We stand and walk in shoes to keep ourselves off the ground. Bare feet are dirtied by touching the ground.

The top girl's feet or shoes are frequently touching the other girl's sides, sometimes even wedged underneath the girl's back or butt for more control. Forced to endure this position, the bottom girl is driven to feel inferior. In contrast, the top girl is kept up off the ground by *using* the other girl as her seat.

But more than that, she sits on an invaluable chair—a living girl.

She has rarely, if ever, sat on something so important, valued, and precious before. All the objects, including animals, she may have sat on before draw no comparison to the priceless chair she sits on now. This prize lifts her psychologically.

Other people who sit on invaluable chairs are called royalty. They sit on thrones. They have historically *ruled* over many people.

Imagine if you sat on a chair made of velvet soft cushions, a solid gold frame, studded with diamonds and rubies that gave you power to throw lightning bolts at your enemy.

How would other people look at you? How would you feel?

If the bottom girl is popular, beautiful, or exceptional in other ways such as in talent, intelligence, or high self-esteem, then the seat is elevated in importance. This is an even rarer circumstance of the top girl sitting on such a powerful and influential person. She relishes in the satisfaction of having mounted and controlled such a prime girl.

She finally feels she has bested this talented, beautiful, alpha girl.

Conversely, if the top girl is less popular, beautiful, intelligent, or talented than the bottom girl, the bottom girl feels more humiliated. This is due to her having allowed herself to be dominated by someone who she thought of as inferior to herself.

4 SENSUAL DYNAMICS

The one who manipulates the other girl's senses has a psychological advantage, in addition to any physical advantage gained.

For the tactile sense, the girl who inflicts more pain and discomfort has the edge.

The unending pressure of the top girl's weight creates a constant tactile experience for the bottom girl. This can lead to feelings of helplessness, hopelessness, and claustrophobia—all states of weakness.

If the top girl simply bounces her weight—a low energy expenditure—she can inflict a variety of hurt to the bottom girl. These may include painful stresses on her ribcage, grinding ribs together, or breaking ribs with a high enough bounce, such as from a standing position. But high bounces risk her adversary escaping. (However, when she first jumps on top of her enemy, this may be a devastating first blow.)

If she bounces on the belly, she crushes stomach and guts, pressuring the bladder and abdomen. The bounces can also expel needed breath of the bottom girl, controlling her very rhythm of breathing. This will also affect her ability to speak clearly since speech requires breath. People may laugh at her broken speech, adding humiliation.

Each bounce from the top girl causes facial expressions of pain from the girl underneath. Yet to the top girl, these bounces are springy and soft. The cushion-like body of the bottom girl conveys vulnerability and harmlessness, driving up the top girl's confidence.

The girls' opposing sensations create two impressions in their minds. One is that the bottom girl is weak and breakable. The other is that the top girl is strong, hardened, and dangerous.

The top girl feels herself sinking *into* the bottom girl, claiming ownership through invasion with her very body. She feels the bottom girl's powerlessness and inability to move in opposition of her force and weight. She feels herself driving down her opponent. She literally squashes her enemy. This elevates her sense of well-being, having so much control.

Even without bounces, just her physical contact against the bottom girl creates a psychological edge because touch can lead to pain—and both girls know this at a primal level. The top girl holds this advantage because besides the constant pressure from her body weight, and besides her legs and feet surrounding her adversary through touch, the ground becomes an extension of herself. It steadily pushes *up* at her adversary as she pushes down. Her body and the ground confine her enemy in a vice grip.

The bottom girl may put her hands on the other girl's thighs or knees simply for a sense of control, but with no real power. Although it reminds her of times when she had power from holding onto things. Psychologically, this holding onto the other's thighs that are uncomfortably invading her space may help her feel as though she has at least some power.

The top girl may rest her hands on her thighs as well, accentuating that she owns and has control over that power—her thighs—which holds her enemy down.

If the bottom girl lies head-first on a downward sloping hill, she has a vulnerable feeling of being slightly upside down, blood rushing to her head, greater difficulty swallowing, greater chance of acid reflux.

One remaining threat to the top girl is a bite from her adversary. Her hands and forearms will be difficult to bite because they can move faster than her opponent's head. Her thighs are very difficult to bite because they are so thick compared to a mouth. The top girl could easily punch her enemy's head back down if it got too close.

And if the bottom girl ever did bite, she would risk inciting her enemy's wrath. This is akin to biting someone with a gun. The top girl is more dangerous to the bottom girl than the reverse. The bottom girl may make her situation worse by a short lived bite.

The higher girl has greater accuracy to spit at the other's face. She can simply let it drip from her mouth when her head is directly above her enemy. When the bottom girl spits upwards, it is pulled down because of gravity and often lands back on herself.

The face is a vulnerable, intimate area of violation where all five senses are active, so more psychologically profound than say an arm or stomach.

The top girl's saliva may smell or taste disgusting. This saliva will create a sensation of wetness caused by the top girl. This informs the bottom girl that she has less control over her tactile sense than her enemy.

Gravity will pull off wet saliva that is spit at the top girl's face faster because her face is vertical rather than horizontal. Even if the bottom girl blinks before spit hits her eyes, when she opens them, the saliva can still drip in. Because another's saliva is often considered gross, it is a form of degradation as well.

The top girl's saliva is also considered part of the top girl. This means that the top girl has placed an additional item that she owns on the bottom girl, increasing ownership over her enemy.

The more one can leave of oneself on an object, space, or another person, the more that person claims ownership over them. This begins with the top girl's body itself, then leaving her scent, then her saliva, and even her feelings of anger through visible bruising or bleeding she caused. If she gets one of her friends on top as well, ownership of her enemy becomes even less disputed.

These dynamics explain the reason a person spits on their enemy in a fight or on the ground as a territorial claim.

The girl on top may have another tactile advantage. Fighting causes body heat to rise. Cooling is essential. Cooling oneself is more difficult when heat is applied to the chest/stomach and sides (the core of a person) as opposed to the extremities of the legs and the crotch area of the girl on top. If it is a hot day and the pavement is hot, the bottom girl will be at a greater disadvantage from heat radiating from the cement. The sensation of heat can add to a claustrophobic feeling. She could actually burn her skin on a very hot day.

Conversely, if there is snow on the ground or the ground is very cold, the bottom girl will be cooled too quickly and may shiver, diminishing her energy.

Sharp stones, broken glass, nails, thorns, rusted metal cans, or simply uneven surfaces on the ground create painful sensations underneath the bottom girl. Much more of her body touches the ground compared to simply her opponent's calves and feet. And if the sharp object is located underneath both girls, their combined weight drives it more forcefully into the bottom girl.

Puddles create tactile discomfort for the bottom girl, especially around the head. The threat of drowning looms. Water may soak her hair or clothes around the core of her body, giving a soppy, cold feeling. As clothes become wet, they can turn transparent and tight, causing humiliation. The liquid may be dirty and enter her orifices, causing more discomfort or disgust, bringing home her inferior position.

Insects may be crawling on the ground with greater access to the bottom girl's more sensitive places such as the head and crotch. An ant, bee, or cockroach crawling into her ear, eye, mouth, nose, or up her skirt can be very traumatic, especially if she cannot prevent it. Simply being bitten or stung by insects near these sensitive areas can be terrifying.

The top girl's sweat may drip down or hair may dangle into the bottom girl's eyes, forcing her to close her eyes and endure these tactile discomforts.

The top girl has a greater visual ability to locate and fetch items from the ground. Dirt, grass, mud, dog feces, water, insects, rotting food, and rocks may be easily thrown down, dropped onto, or smashed into the bottom girl's face and body, creating a variety of disturbing tactile sensations.

The top girl has greater ability to force the other girl to taste things by shoving them into her mouth. Remember, her head is less mobile and can be fixed between the other girl's knees or thighs. When the top girl controls what the bottom girl tastes, it psychologically increases the top girl's dominance.

The more objectionable the taste, the more

profound the act. These tastes can be anything close by, such as rotting food, mud, dirt, worms, bugs, dog feces, dirty water, etc. The tastes can also be psychologically intense if they come from the top girl herself, such as her saliva, sweat, or nasal mucus.

The sense of smell is the most primal, profound sense that we have. It responds to pheromones which we cannot even consciously detect.

If there is any truth to women living or working together becoming more in sync with their menstruation cycles, it is believed to be done by smell.

Our sense of smell can identify body odor from sweat, urine, and feces. With some people on a bad day, you don't have to get closer than six feet from them to smell these stenches.

But in a fight, you are *intimately* close to your opponent.

Animals often mark their territory by defecating and urinating around an area. The power of such soils is in the intense, personal smells they leave which persist for days. Even domesticated, trained cats will sometimes deposit their urine and feces at a disputed area of territory to mark it as theirs.

In some extreme cases, an emotionally distraught child may wipe his feces on the walls when placed in a time out or is upset for another reason. Some monkeys wipe or throw their feces around their cage when upset. Serial killers sometimes urinate or wipe their feces on their victims. Please explain the above if not to mark territory or ownership on an animalistic level, attempting to gain power.

Animals also may rub their body against objects to deposit their odors. One's odor then claims ownership over an area, object, another animal, or sometimes a person.

A cat rubs against you, the door, or another animal, not always to scratch itself or be petted, but often to mark its territory or ownership of another.

If you are female, think of when you smelled a rival girl's scent on a guy you were dating. How did that make you feel? Did it spark some jealousy? Maybe she just hugged him in a friendly way, or accidently brushed up against him. But didn't it seem like she marked her territory in a way?

Sexual activity also exchanges bodily smells to a high degree, marking people's mates as their territory.

Perhaps you have had the experience of loaning another girl a pair of your shorts or a top, causing them to smell badly. Afterwards, did you wear them without washing them? Probably not, especially if you didn't like the girl or weren't close friends. You wanted them to be clean and smell fresh. A type of ownership occurs when we soil something.

People slip and cannot be perfect in regards to cleanliness. Even after urinating and wiping the area dry, urine can still drip out as you walk back to class or work. Freeing the anus area of particles of feces isn't always feasible after a bowel movement.

Sometimes cleanliness can be exceptionally difficult such as when women don't shave or lack razors so that hair growth in the pubic and anus region collects urine, sweat, and feces. Other factors include having just exercised, run out of toilet paper, sweating more on a hot day, had recent sex in which sperm has been deposited inside or around the vagina area, having menstruation, diarrhea, a yeast infection, or a sexually transmitted disease.

These can create strong stenches.

Or simply a girl's laziness with hygiene creates stenches.

If she skipped a shower, used the bathroom in a rushed manner of not thoroughly wiping herself, did not have a spare tampon or pad to swap the old one with, or wore used clothing that day, she will smell worse.

Although it may be somewhat socially unacceptable to think of women in these unclean ways, the truth is that we are not perfect.

Natural smells are a part of our animalistic nature.

We try to erase these smells with deodorants, perfumes, and oils, but our smells mix with the artificial ones anyways, creating our own unique fragrance, not bought in any store.

The top girl's soiled—to some degree—crotch and anus are posed above and rub against her rival. This creates the primal impact of owning this girl. The more the bottom girl struggles, the more her enemy' worst scents distribute over her body, marking her as the top girl's territory.

Because of the heated battle and her opponent's

warm body below, the top girl may sweat more on her legs and in her crotch and anus areas, intensifying her scent on her enemy. And the longer she sits there, the more fixed her scents become on her opponent.

Women's sense of smell is greater than men's. Females actually have more cells in the olfactory bulb, a place in the brain dedicated to sense of smell.

So this dynamic of ownership by smell is greater in female fights.

Though the pinned girl may not be consciously thinking of her enemy's scents, they still impact her nonetheless. (An example was discussed earlier with a person's pheromones, which cannot be detected even when we consciously try to smell them. Yet they still have dramatic impacts on mood and behavior.)

The top girl's odors intensify to her opponent if she sits on the chest. Her legs and crotch surround her opponent's nose. If she pulls up on the person's hair, the person's face will be in her crotch. The inner thighs are also places of increased sweating and stronger body odor. If the bottom girl turns her head, her nose will be against an inner thigh.

In this position, there is no escaping the top girl's personal smells. If she leans or falls forward, her stomach and navel will be in her opponent's face and her breasts and underarms will fall above her opponent's hair, essentially encapsulating the bottom girl's head with key areas that emit odor. For the bottom girl, her enemy's scent is everywhere, psychologically ensnaring her.

Familiar scents are comforting to us. The bottom girl's own scent is comforting to her, as well as those of her loved ones. But she is *losing* her scent. Even worse, she is immersed in the foreign world of her enemy's scents.

As the top girl looks down at her adversary underneath her crotch and anus, she is likely aware that this person is trapped in the same area of her most intimate and smelliest odors. These are scents that are familiar to the top girl, scents that she exclusively owns, scents that help define her, and scents which she has carried with her every day of her life.

They are hers. Her enemy now suffers them.

She may become smug. She has forced the bottom girl to know her at the intimate, primal level of smell. She has also deposited her stink onto her enemy, invisibly marking the opponent as hers.

These aromatic trespasses on the bottom girl create more discomfort, humiliation, and disgust for her. To be unable to escape the foulest smells of her adversary weakens her sense of strength and confidence.

The top girl's hair, which is odor intensive, often dangles close to or on the bottom girl's face.

This is another difference between girl and guy fights, as girls are more likely to have long hair which carries more odor. It drags along the shoulders, neck, and arms all day long, picking up oils and smells, as well as creating its own.

The top girl's feet often touch the other's body. These frequently have odor or are at least associated with dirtiness. Again, because the bottom girl is forced to endure this, it displays the top girl's dominance.

And girls are more likely than guys to have bare feet in a fight. Guys almost never wear high heels. Due to the difficulty of fighting in high heels, girls either kick these shoes off before the fight or the shoes easily fall off during the fight.

Other shoes girls frequently wear include slip-on type shoes or strappy shoes, whereas guys often wear tennis shoes or similar type shoes that are rugged and firmly affixed to the feet.

If the top girl wears a skirt or short dress, her body odor travels more freely. If the material covers the bottom girl's face, it not only traps the air from the crotch area to the bottom girl's nose, but also transmits scent from the material itself of the top girl.

If the top girl wears a loose shirt and leans forward, it may hang over the other girl's face, material which has been literally soaked with the top girl's sweat and stench throughout the day.

Understand that these are not simply smells from a friend or even just another girl, but smells from an arch enemy. This creates a greater harm than one may initially comprehend.

Smell and memory are highly linked together, but especially in the midst of strong emotions. These can be painful or happy emotions.

An example of a happy coupling of memory and smell might be Grandma's chocolate chip cookies baking in the oven as a child. When you smell the same cookies in the present, a flood of those happy times with Grandma come back. Or perhaps a loved one has died, and months later you smell a shirt they used to wear, bringing back the good memories and closeness of them.

An example of a negative coupling of memory and smell can be observed in rape. The victim can be triggered into a flashback of the horrid memory simply by a similar smell in the present of that past event.

The bottom girl is impacted at a deep psychological level with her enemy's smell. The stench becomes bound with the trauma from the fight.

This coupling leaves a mental imprint of her enemy that feels something like: *my scent hurts you; it comes with my domineering violence. These have occurred together. My scent and conquest of you are part of the same force. Whenever you smell me again, you will be reminded of your failure today. You will be submissive, as you are now.*

In the future, the invisible power of the top girl's smell will be confusing and inexplicable to the bottom girl. All she will notice is that she turns submissive when the top girl comes close. This can be infuriating to her sense of control.

The bottom girl's vision can be blinded by the sun or lamps above. Yet this provides better sight for her adversary.

If she is lying on high grass, her vision is cloistered by the long shafts, giving a claustrophobic, everything-is-closing-in type of feeling.

If it is raining, snowing, hailing, or windy, her eyes will be pelted with falling substances, while the top girl's vision is much less hindered.

Animals frequently make themselves appear bigger by stretching out their feathers or limbs to give the impression of a greater threat.

Because the top girl's legs are spread wide, it creates a psychological illusion that her entire body is larger.

By sliding forward to the chest, the top girl's size *increases* to the bottom girl. This can be quite frightening to the girl underneath. She can no longer see her own body. Her vision is filled instead with her enemy, who is now larger and more intimidating.

The top girl's thighs are so close that they appear enormously thick. Her head towers in the sky. Her breasts (a private area for females) are or almost are above the other's head. Her crotch and belly are magnified.

With female fights in particular, the top girl's hips appear incredibly wide to her adversary, creating the sense of a greater threat.

She literally overwhelms the bottom girl's sense of vision. In almost every direction possible, the bottom girl is forced to see only her enemy. The top girl's intimidating appearance gives the impression of great strength and dominance.

As her enemy's legs, hips, crotch, and body surround her head, the bottom girl has the sensation of everything closing in around her. Claustrophobic fear is common.

Her enemy's crotch enlarges and is humiliating for her to be so close to see it in such detail. She may begin to fear an assault of a sexual nature simply because of her position.

People are usually not privy to this sight and proximity. The bottom girl becomes more aware of her enemy's owned area forced onto her and holding her down.

If the top girl wears a skirt, short dress, short shorts, or tight form-fitting shorts or leggings, the bottom girl may see more humiliating details.

These dynamics are mostly exclusive to female fights because males hardly ever wear these types of exposing clothes.

If the top girl wears a short skirt or short dress, then her naked legs, bare parts of the buttocks, underpants, and skin around the crotch may be touching her adversary. In rare circumstances, the top girl may not even be wearing underpants.

Skin on skin contact is much more intimate than contact with another person's clothing. An actual organ of your enemy is touching you: her skin. It has hairs, oils, sweat, and she can feel you to a higher degree from this more intimate contact.

These conditions of sight and touch create a much

greater private personal space. Remember, personal space is delineated by sight and touch, not just smell.

The bottom girl forced to endure her enemy's greater private space causes her to feel a greater humiliation. This grants her enemy greater ownership over her. This deep type of domination from private space is not found in fights with less exposed skin and body parts, of which is more common in guy fights.

An example may help elucidate this. If you are a heterosexual guy, imagine wrestling another guy that is your enemy while he is wearing a short skirt with skimpy tight underwear, and has entirely bare legs and feet. It doesn't feel so good, does it? It is likely more humiliating and revolting if he sits on your chest and you see a bulge from his sexual organs through the underwear.

This dynamic also occurs in girl fights.

Now put the top guy in a short shirt that exposes his midriff with two string straps over his bare shoulders. This isn't making it any more comfortable for the bottom guy, is it?

For the top girl, her enemy appears like a small, defenseless child. The bottom girl is low on the ground, and at most, only her upper body and head can be seen—a dwarfed image of her. If the top girl sits on her chest, only her neck and head can be seen.

This psychologically empowers the top girl. She is used to having physical power over smaller people. Younger (smaller) children are also expected to listen to older (larger) people.

Staring is an act of domination.

A staring contest is more easily won by the top girl. After all, her enemy looks so puny and harmless. Whereas the bottom girl sees her enemy as scarily enormous, so she may give in more easily to looking away. Also, she may be forced to blink or look away because of particles, sweat, or hair falling into her eyes. Losing a staring contest is a submissive gesture.

After winning, the top girl has the ease of simply moving her head to see something other than the puny bottom girl. Her sense of vision is not filled with her enemy.

She feels so comfortable in her position—her enemy being less a threat—that she may feel free to look around at other things. She doesn't need to constantly watch the bottom girl anymore. Because if the bottom girl tried to get away, the top girl would easily feel it through her sense of touch.

The bottom girl's eyes will tend to be more fixed on parts of the top girl, trying to control the threats through vision.

The bottom girl's face is looking up, which is a less powerful position than the top girl's. To be able to scan the horizon, you can observe additional threats coming. But to only look up, you miss out on this. The top girl can look in many different directions around her by turning her head. The bottom girl can only look in a few, which are mostly blocked by the top girl's body. This is a disadvantage for protection at an animalistic level.

Dirt, sand, grass, or other particles kicked up during the fight are more likely to fall into the bottom girl's eyes which look upwards, as well as other things discussed before. These things can temporarily blind her to punches.

If the top girl squeezes her thighs against the sides of bottom girl's head, the thighs block more of the bottom girl's vision. This not only involves the tactile, visual, and olfactory senses, but also compromises the bottom girl's auditory sense. The thighs close off the ears ability to gather sound.

This creates a frightening loss for the bottom girl. With impaired hearing, she may not be as aware of potential bystanders who may help or harm her. She will have more difficulty hearing potential dangers, encouragements, warnings, or threats.

The top girl can hinder the other's ability to utter sound. Putting something into or covering the bottom girl's mouth can accomplish this. She will have difficulty yelling for help, warning others if she is in too much pain, convincing the top girl to relent and get off, or threatening the top girl.

Verbal communication is a powerful tool in a social society. To have this sacrificed is a psychological loss as well.

The top girl has better use of her hands to control the bottom girl's facial language by twisting and manipulating the skin and muscles of the face. This is more likely to be seen in a play fight. The top girl can use her hands to scrunch the bottom girl's cheeks and erase the bottom girl's nonverbal facial communication of confidence or strength. She can also manipulate the face to appear ugly—a social weakness.

5 EMOTIONAL VARIABLES

A person's feelings are psychological impacts.

Anger can be directed at others or yourself. When it is directed at one's self, it is called guilt.

If one girl feels guilty, the other has a distinct advantage. A girl who directs anger at herself will most likely *not even want* to win. She will feel she deserves to be punished—the result of her anger being directed at herself. The other girl will see this as weakness and use it to her advantage.

Even if the guilty girl chooses to defend herself, her self-loathing will cause her not feel worthy at key points in the fight to take control in which just a moment's hesitation will affect the outcome. Her anger at herself makes her feel like a bad person. Because of that, her ability to harm/dominate another person—even in defense of herself—is perceived by her as wrong and unjustified.

In contrast, the girl who directs anger outward sees the other person as guilty and deserving to be punished. The other person is perceived as bad. She will quickly capitalize on *any* opportunity to hurt this person. She sees herself as a victim who needs to be protected and provided retribution.

This is a reason for conversation preceding a fight, attempting to make the opponent feel guilt: "You slut! You slept with my boyfriend."

Once a girl is pinned, her psychological state changes.

Her vulnerable position and dependence on another's compassion brings her back to childhood, when she was small, powerless, and dependent on adults. This is a weakened psychological state of vulnerability. She was supposed to respect, obey, and take guidance from the bigger, more powerful and knowledgeable adults. This may stir old feelings of hurt if she had been abused by adults. The top girl's overbearing weight and visual size resonates as an adult and encourages childhood submission from the bottom girl.

The girl who feels more hurt, depression, or humiliation is also at a disadvantage, as these are weak states.

The girl who feels more anger directed outward has a physical and psychological edge, as this prepares the body to be stronger (this is true in untrained fighters; however high anger in trained fighters can hinder mental functioning for complex fighting maneuvers). Fear also prepares the body to run or fight, but it is a psychologically weaker state than anger.

With fear you believe that you will likely be hurt soon, so can act more desperate, impulsive, and subservient.

The bottom girl is more susceptible to extreme fear or panic attacks. These create decreased mental functioning, faster heart rate, increased sweating, hyperventilation, uselessly draining away her energy.

Panic attacks may make the girl's vision unclear, create dizziness, lightheadedness, trembling, shaking, numbness in her hands, chest pains, feeling as though she can't breathe and is dying. She will have a sense that something unimaginably horrible is about to occur and that she is powerless to prevent it, and be consumed with a desperate need to escape.

Under normal conditions a panic attack is one of the worst psychological conditions to experience. But being trapped underneath an enemy, the panic advances to extreme levels.

The top girl forces a type of empathy on her enemy in which her enemy now suffers as she once had. She pursues this either directly or indirectly to feel heard and understood. With this understanding, she may believe on some level that her enemy will learn a lesson not to hurt her again.

The bottom girl will feel humiliation.

Even if she is in denial at the moment, she will feel humiliated at a later time when her psychological defenses eventually erode. This feeling stems not just from her forced submission, not just from her presentation of weakness and failure in the fight, but also from her sexually submissive position.

She has been mounted by her enemy.

The bottom girl's personal space has been invaded not simply by another person, but by another person's sexual organs.

Her opponent's legs are spread open upon her. She feels the other's warm genitals and anus pressing against her, and possibly catches scent of them.

The top girl may threaten, "I can do whatever I want, bitch." And even if the top girl has no sexual intention behind the threat, the bottom girl's mind is easily inclined in that direction simply because of her position.

She is lying on her back, the most common sexual position for a female. And her opponent is also in a common, yet dominant female sexual position—straddling another person or object. The bottom girl's head may be only inches from her adversary's vagina—inches and one to two layers of clothing from an oral sex position. The sight of her opponent's crotch is almost unavoidable.

Also, the sexual nature is generally greater in a female fight due to reasons previously discussed in which females wear clothing and shoes that exposes more of their bodies. Females also have two main sexual private areas on their bodies as opposed to males' single one.

These differences mean that female fights have generally more observed bare skin, more skin on skin contact, more detailed views of covered body parts due to tighter clothing, as well as double the sexual areas that are above the bottom opponent in this type of pin.

The top girl has mounted, controls, and rides the other's body, experiencing pleasure from these advantages.

When she looks down, she sees the other person underneath her sex organs, where a partner, finger, vibrator, pillow, or her imagination has aroused her in the past. Even if she never intended to exploit this sexually dominant position with her opponent, it is hers.

It is the reason some girls hesitate to sit on and straddle another. It is usually not feminine or socially acceptable to be seen in such an indecent position, but perhaps most acceptable in a fight. In fact, some burgeoning lesbians strike up play fights simply to enjoy this position with a girl with the least social resistance.

Bystanders may exemplify this lewd position with their exclamations, "Rape!" "Oouu!" or "That just looks wrong!" In a play fight, the bottom girl may jokingly exclaim, "Help me! I'm being raped!"

Inhibited girl fighters will first put their knee on the other girl, lie across her body, sit sideways on her, or kneel beside her before they finally abandon their inhibition and take the more advantageous position of straddling her.

Even after taking this position, they may still feel uncomfortable to the point of getting off the bottom girl too soon. This often leads to continued fighting because the bottom girl had not given up.

Some places in the world even outlaw women straddling a motorcycle, and require them to sit *sideways* on it.

Please explain this.

This makes no safety sense at all. In fact, it is downright dangerous. A female rider can easily slip off and hurt herself. The only way this sexual discrimination makes sense is that women straddling an object appears sexual or is sexual, and the people of that culture don't want women to be seen in that way.

In European history, it was indecent for women to straddle a horse as women do today; but it was acceptable to sit sidesaddle on the animal.

If you still doubt at this point that one girl straddling another is sexual, then I may never convince you.

However, you may convince yourself. You can ask one female to do it to another in a crowd. This usually works best in a crowd that has their verbal inhibitions lowered, such as through alcohol or a large gathering of close friends. If the women agree, you can listen to other people's reactions for yourself.

You can listen to a crowd's reactions when a woman rides a mechanical bull at a bar. Or listen to the reactions when one woman sits astride another in Jell-O, oil, or mud wrestling.

Or, you can imagine a strange female jumping on top of your supine boyfriend. How would you feel? Why would you feel that way? Is there something more sexual about it than just sitting beside him? What is that?

Power is an aphrodisiac. The top girl's position of dominance is mentally stimulating for her. She is comforted that she has gained power over her adversary.

From the passion of battle, the top girl's animal side is closer to the surface. Fighting is a carnal, animalistic act, and the leap to another carnal desire is closer than before the fight.

The social inhibitions to physically fight have already been broken. As such, other inhibitions become less intense.

The top girl's sexual organs are touching the wriggling, warm body below, and they may become stimulated. Although this is not common and more likely in play fighting in which pins are usually longer and a positive emotional connection exists between the girls.

Some women even report sexual arousal or orgasm while riding a horse, motorcycle, roller coaster, or bicycle. Some while sitting on a washing machine or a car seat with bass speakers booming underneath. Female anatomy is different than males. These differences contribute to different frequencies with the ways of being stimulated. Closer similarities between the two sexes may include reports of arousal or orgasm while climbing and descending a rope or doing stomach exercises at the gym.

The top girl may reflexively squeeze her legs and feet against her opponent to get a better grip on her opponent's struggles at escape. Her lower stomach and back muscles will work to keep herself stabilized on her opponent's bucks, turns, and twists. This increase of blood to the pelvic area combined with contact with or by the clitoris increases the chance of arousal.

This would be a natural physiological response. A similar uncontrollable female response sometimes occurs in the violence of rape. The victim often feels betrayed by her own body because of the arousal.

Although the top girl may have no sexual intent or plan, the threat looms in the back of the bottom girl's mind. This is especially true with longer pins, as the bottom girl wonders why her opponent is just sitting there and questions what the girl is getting out of it.

People reach for whatever strength they can in a physical fight, including with words. The top girl may guess the bottom girl's fears and make sexually derogative comments like, "How does my cunt smell?"

The top girl can observe the humiliation on the bottom girl's face, recognizing the weakened state and escalating her confidence.

The bottom girl may observe or imagine arousal

on her opponent's face, suffering further humiliation. The more she struggles to free herself, the more her body rubs against her adversary's genitalia. This causes additional humiliation and a no-win situation.

Even if she lies still, her rapid breathing can create waves of pressure on or close to her opponent's clitoris. From the physical exertion of the fight, the rise and fall of her chest and stomach will be forceful and fast before they tire. The bottom girl's body feels warm to the top girl straddling it. The bottom girl's rhythmic, hard heartbeats can often be felt by the top girl.

The bottom girl may feel the growing heat from the top girl's stimulated genitals, adding more humiliation.

Beyond that, the deepest part of the top girl claims ownership over the bottom girl. Her sexual feelings have arisen on her enemy, creating a sense of capturing and surrounding her adversary—as they might a loved partner—at a most intimate level.

She has created a greater private space of hers on her enemy, directed from her intense private feelings.

An animal, such as a dog, often demonstrates dominance by mounting, thrusting with stomach contractions, and, in the case of a female, rubbing her genitals against another.

Even if the top girl is not aroused, she may purposely bounce, grind, or thrust her pelvis into the bottom girl as an act of sexual domination. She may also rock forwards and backwards in a repetitive manner. These acts are more likely in a play fight, accompanied by much laughter from the obvious social taboos being breached.

Because the bottom girl lacks the power to stop these sexual acts, she may try turning her head away to attempt to avoid them as best as she can. This at least prevents her from seeing her adversary's facial expression of superiority, confidence, and arousal.

However, the turning away out of discomfort is a submissive gesture.

These sexual violations with words or grinding in real fights breach the bottom girl's emotional and physical boundaries. To say the least, they are invasions into her personal space which increase her psychological discomfort. As this closeness is unwanted, it is a violation of intimacy. It conveys exploitation of her against her will for the top girl's own satisfaction and desires, having a rape-like quality.

The bottom girl's humiliation is increased if these acts are done in front of a crowd, adding the hurt of social debasement. Frequently, the crowd holds electronic devices (cell phones with cameras and video recording capabilities) which can record the fight to be placed on the internet, expanding the number of people who can observe the bottom girl's submission and degradation, escalating her humiliation.

6 CROWD PHENOMENON

People in the crowd perhaps should be objective, but often are not.

Some people in the crowd may see the bottom girl as being weaker than they previously believed. They may lose respect for her. They may think that they can do disrespectful things to her since she can't defend herself well, as evidenced by her loss of the fight.

The top girl has broken a previous social norm of respecting the bottom girl, and with that, allowed space for a new norm to surface: it is okay to hurt the bottom girl.

Alternatively, their respect for the top girl may rise because she has shown her power and what she is willing to do and the extent she will go to for sticking up for herself.

In these ways, the two girls fighting are attached

to the surrounding crowd. Other types of attachment are discussed below.

Girls with low self-esteems may experience vicariously through the dominant girl. In the past, they may have felt powerless against the bottom girl, threatened by her competitive beauty or talent, hurt by her actions and words. But when they see her dominated, they can envision her beneath them or that they are on top and in control at last.

At the least, they can envision the bottom girl as vulnerable and easily taken advantage of in this moment. They may yell things at her that they wouldn't dare say at other times.

Guys with low self-esteems may also live vicariously through the dominant female. They can envision that they are top. They may have repressed desires of dominating females. These feelings at last can be expressed secondhand through the girl on top. Or the fact that the bottom girl is vulnerable may be seen as a step toward opportunity to take advantage of her, perhaps looking or taking pictures up her skirt, or at least allowing their imaginations to run wild with this girl's vulnerable position. Maybe they will try to make fun of her at a later time as an attempt to control her.

Dependent people can relate to the bottom girl. They have felt the same way, being dominated themselves by people and life circumstances. Their hurt and anger over this powerlessness may be expressed at the top girl. They may yell at her and fight to get her off.

Some bystanders have been hurt in the past by a person being irresponsible, weak, indecisive, and ineffective. Maybe some have an alcoholic parent with whom they can't express their feelings, the parent being powerless against his addiction. As they watch the bottom girl's weakness and ineffective struggling, they might transfer their angry feelings onto her to feel empowered themselves. They might encourage the top girl to punch, control, and hurt the bottom girl more. Or they might physically help the top girl to sustain the pin or hurt the bottom girl. They are still angry at their parent and transferring this onto the weak girl in the fight.

We are all in daily struggles in life. These may be struggles to get social status, better jobs, better relationships, greater income, beauty, intelligence, compassion, physical health, strength, talent, independence, and power over our internal demons. It would be nice to just be dominant in these struggles, winning, but often we fail to some degree. Thus, we have feelings of hurt and loss.

Simply watching a girl fight (or any sport for that matter), crowd members can displace these feelings onto the winner or loser as a means to feel more in control themselves.

Their long held feelings of powerlessness, hurt, and anger may be finally dealt with vicariously.

Recall some soccer games in which the crowd had inexplicably become violent to the players or referees.

Although this understanding may disturb some readers, it explains why even strangers become drawn into, excited about, and verbally involved in the fight. It makes the crowd members come alive, feel at one with themselves, and become pulled into the present moment because they are dealing with their own feelings—despite the displaced manner.

Who knew all these domination and submission dynamics could exist in girl fights?

But really that is the nature of a fight. A struggle between domination and submission.

Being there in the moment, it is difficult to understand everything that transpires. Sometimes you will get caught up in your emotions. A number of psychological underlying forces occur simultaneously and so briefly that conscious awareness of them is difficult. But careful, objective mindfulness can be revealing.

Perhaps this book answers, at least in part, the dynamics of the struggle for dominance in girl fights.

THE END

ABOUT THE AUTHOR

Dean Henryson is the author of the award-winning horror book, *Fierce Peace*, as well as, *A Love in Darkness* and *Imaginary Darkness*. Dean began his writing career with the psychological self-help book, *Be Yourself*. He was born and raised in California. He provides counseling to families and children in Los Angeles County. He also worked as a foster care social worker for many years, becoming inspired to write of the struggles in life.